OUR VOICES
SPANISH AND LATINO FIGURES OF AMERICAN HISTORY™

ÁLVAR NÚÑEZ CABEZA DE VACA

EXPLORER OF THE AMERICAN SOUTHWEST

SANDRA COLMENARES

rosen publishing's
rosen central®

New York

Published in 2020 by The Rosen Publishing Group, Inc.
29 East 21st Street, New York, NY 10010

Library of Congress Cataloging-in-Publication Data

Names: Colmenares, Sandra, author.
Title: Alvar Núñez Cabeza de Vaca : explorer of the American Southwest /
Sandra Colmenares.
Description: First edition. | New York : Rosen Central, 2020. | Series:
Our voices: Spanish and Latino figures of American history | Includes
bibliographical references and index. | Audience: Grades 5–8.
Identifiers: LCCN 2018014360 | ISBN 9781508184270 (library bound) | ISBN
9781508184263 (pbk.)
Subjects: LCSH: Núñez Cabeza de Vaca, Alvar, active 16th century—
Juvenile literature. | Explorers—America—Biography—Juvenile literature.
| Explorers—Spain—Biography—Juvenile literature. | America—Discovery
and exploration—Spanish—Juvenile literature.
Classification: LCC E125.N9 C65 2019 | DDC 970.01/6092 [B]—dc23
LC record available at https://lccn.loc.gov/2018014360

On the cover: Álvar Núñez Cabeza de Vaca, Alonso del Castillo Maldonado,
Andrés Dorantes, and the Arab slave Estevanico were the four survivors of
the adventurous expedition to conquer and settle in La Florida.

CONTENTS

INTRODUCTION

The Spanish conquistador Álvar Núñez Cabeza de Vaca's story is one of the great epics of history. He was many things: hidalgo (an important officer), explorer, and soldier. Not only that, he was a royal official to the Spanish crown during the 1500s, when this European kingdom experienced the most incredible expansion of its power around the known and unknown world.

Cabeza de Vaca, like many hidalgo men of his time, made a living by carrying out the orders and other responsibilities given to him by his lords and the Crown. Like his father, grandfather, and a long line of his ancestors, Cabeza de Vaca was one of history's heroic figures. He helped the Spanish Empire achieve its rule over a great part of Europe as well as a world that was little known until then: the American territory. From the European point of view, this territory was a new world to be discovered.

By the time he was named royal treasurer and second in command in Pánfilo Narváez's expedition, he was already an experienced and distinguished Spanish soldier, noted for his fighting campaigns in Europe, including Spain. He was appointed to explore, conquer, and settle the territory of La Florida in North America, which was unknown territory for the Spanish. At the time, only a few other European explorers had visited the territory that would later become the United States. But Cabeza de Vaca spent eight years wandering this land, taking notes of what he saw and experienced. He later wrote everything he could remember in a document that he called *La Relación*, or *The Relation*. He addressed it to the ruler of the Holy Roman Empire, Charles V.

The Relation was published in Spain for the first time in 1542 and a second time in 1555. But this was by no means the only documentation of these journeys. An earlier document called the *Joint Report* was written in 1536. The *Joint Report* is a thirty-page summary of the journey as drawn up by Cabeza de Vaca,

Cabeza de Vaca and his fellow explorers experienced a difficult journey in the unknown lands of La Florida and the North American territory.

together with Alonso del Castillo and Andrés Dorantes, in Mexico and addressed to the Audiencia of Santo Domingo, which was Spain's first court in America.

As he wandered the North American territory, Cabeza de Vaca learned to love the beautiful land as well as the Native Americans. Although he suffered greatly during this time, he envisioned brotherhood with his fellow humans. He was also determined and willing to bring civilization and Christianity to them. During his journey, Cabeza de Vaca wrote that he learned how to cure the sick, the natives' languages, and how to make peace with the hostile natives.

Although the expedition didn't achieve its goals, Cabeza de Vaca's accounts of the journey depicts an adventure of the first Europeans in an unknown land and how they managed to survive eight long years.

CHAPTER ONE

THE ORIGINS OF ÁLVAR NÚÑEZ CABEZA DE VACA

Historians have searched for evidence about a precise place and date of Cabeza de Vaca's birth for centuries. They have often come up short, however, mainly as a result of a lack of information that supports any one historian's theory. Almost any theory could be possible until exact information is discovered, so a variety of arguments have been generally accepted.

WHEN AND WHERE: THE QUEST FOR A BIRTHPLACE AND DATE

Most theories suggest that Cabeza de Vaca was born in one of three cities: Jerez de los Caballeros, province of Extremadura; Seville; or Jerez de la Frontera, province of Andalusia. All three cities are located in the same region of the southern Iberian Peninsula. One theory states that Jerez de los Caballeros was his birthplace, based on the fact that a large branch of the Cabeza de Vaca family lived there. Some believe that he was born in Seville because of registry documents from 1524 in which he is listed as an inhabitant and working for the house of Medina Sidonia. However, there aren't any other clues to suggest he grew up there.

Cabeza de Vaca may have been born in the Spanish cities of Jerez de la Frontera, located close by the Gulf of Cádiz in the Southwest, or Seville, located a bit farther inland.

Jerez de la Frontera is most likely his birthplace, for two reasons. First, it is the city where his parents are buried. Second, and more convincingly, it is also the place he identifies as his place of origin in his book *La Relación* (*The Relation*).

As for his birth date, historians have only approximate dates because they have not yet found a legal document or registry. Unfortunately, Cabeza de Vaca did not write about it in *La Relación*. Most historical literature agrees that he might have been born between 1485 and 1495.

"HEAD OF A COW"

In *La Relación*, Cabeza de Vaca writes that he is the son of Francisco de Vera and Doña Teresa Cabeza de Vaca, and grandson of Pedro de Vera "who conquered the Canaries." His own name, Álvar Núñez Cabeza de Vaca, comes from his mother. It is in honor of two relatives with the same name: his mother's uncle and her great-grandfather. For reasons that remain unknown, he preferred Cabeza de Vaca, which means "head of a cow" in Spanish, more than the name Núñez.

One theory is that he was drawn to the history and legend of this name. In a popular Castilian tale from the thirteenth century, a shepherd called Martín Alhaja left a sign that directed the Christian army to a passage through the mountains of Sierra Morena. This allowed seventy thousand Christian soldiers to launch a surprise attack and defeat the Moors' army, even though they were outnumbered by one hundred thousand soldiers. The sign that changed the war was a cow skull mounted on a stake. Thus, on July 16, 1212, the Christians won the decisive clash remembered as the Battle of Las Navas de Tolosa. Soon after, the story continues, King Alfonso VIII of Castile honored Alhaja with a knight's

In the Battle of Las Navas de Tolosa (1212), Christian troops surprise and defeat the Moors. The royal title "Cabeza de Vaca" may have originated in this critical clash.

title and named him "Cabeza de Vaca." It's hard to say whether or not this story is true. Cabeza de Vaca's ancestors did participate in the seven-hundred-year-long wars known as Reconquista in Spanish, however, in which they reconquered the Iberian Peninsula from Moorish domination.

CASTILIAN SOCIETY AND ECONOMY

In the sixteenth century, strong social hierarchies and traditional structure dominated the Castilian society and economy. At the head of society was Queen Isabella. Below her were a small number of titled nobles who served her as vassals and warlords. They were followed by a large number of *caballeros* (knights) and hidalgos below them. All these groups made up the kingdom's nobility. At the bottom of that pyramid were the peasants, which included artisans.

The economy was based on land ownership. Artisans rented land to cultivate and paid dues to their lords. The peasants made up about 80 percent of the entire population. The titled nobles owned about 97 percent of the land in Queen Isabella's kingdom. They paid the queen their own tribute as her vassals. The hidalgos served as vassals to the titled nobles by providing military services. They made their fortunes through that service with the spoils of their conquered territories. For many centuries,

(continued on the next page)

(continued from the previous page)

their service consisted of fighting the Moors and expanding the Spanish kingdom on the Iberian Peninsula and beyond.

During Cabeza de Vaca's time, Spain was made up of two major kingdoms. The Castile kingdom was ruled by Isabella, and the Aragon kingdom was ruled by Ferdinand II. Ferdinand II and Isabella married in 1469. In 1494, Pope Alexander VI coined the title *Reyes Católicos*, or Catholic Monarchs, in recognition of various accomplishments, including the reconquest of Granada, the last Muslim settlement in Spain, from the Moors (1481–1492); their New World discovery (1492); their efforts to convert the Jewish people of Spain to Christianity (1492); and, of course, their strong bonds to the Catholic Church.

Isabella of Castile and Ferdinand II of Aragon, illustrated here, married in 1469, and ruled their kingdoms together as well as establishing an empire in the New World.

A LINEAGE OF CONQUERORS

It's likely that Cabeza de Vaca grew up hearing stories about how the Moors, the Muslims from northern Africa, had invaded his homeland centuries ago and how Christian armies had been pushing them back for centuries. In fact, his father and grandfather, along with other ancestors, had been involved in the *Reconquista* from the time that the Moors expanded their control and power from northern Africa. The Christian states in the Iberian Peninsula were determined to recapture the territory from the Moors and establish Christianity as the sole religion and culture.

Pedro de Vera y Mendoza was Cabeza de Vaca's grandfather. He served the Spanish crown in the later years of the Reconquista in many forms. He worked as a supplier to the royal armies, as well as a government official for several communities on the peninsula. He also helped conquer the Canary Islands. Like many hidalgos of his generation and position, Pedro de Vera was encouraged by the *capitulaciones*, a type of royal contract between Queen Isabella and hidalgos to conquer new territories for the Spanish crown and Christianity. In exchange, the hidalgos received money and a reward and were granted a noble title. In 1481, after six years of wars for the Grand Canaria, Pedro de Vera conquered the island and was appointed to the position of its military governor.

Cabeza de Vaca may have greatly admired his grandfather's bravery and probably had heard some of the stories directly from him. There's little doubt that Cabeza de Vaca wanted to follow in his grandfather's footsteps and become a conquistador and colonial governor. In fact, on his second expedition to America, many years later, he named a territory he conquered in what is now Brazil "the province of de Vera" to honor his grandfather. Cabeza de Vaca's father and grandfather died around 1506, and his mother a few years after, in 1509.

According to legal documents, by the 1520s, Cabeza de Vaca had married María Marmolejo. She was from a wealthy converso family, or a Jewish family that adopted Christianity, from Seville. It's unknown if they ever had children.

EARLY SERVICE TO THE HOUSE OF MEDINA SIDONIA

In 1503, Cabeza de Vaca began his service to his family's overlord, the duke of the House of Medina Sidonia, together with his three younger brothers and a cousin. He might have been between eleven and eighteen years old at the time. He served the house for twenty-four years: as cavallero de Jerez (1503), as page (1513), and as camarero, or chamberlain (1519). As a chamberlain, he had the combined duties of a man-of-arms, administrative assistant, and gentleman in waiting. The house of the duke of Medina Sidonia was one of the most powerful houses in Castile, dominating the municipal government in Seville. The Medina Sidonia also owned armed ships and used them for privateering and international trade, as well as in military battles for the Spanish Empire. The practice of privateering was similar to that of the pirates, but the privateers had the benefit of being protected by their governments. When they attacked enemy ships—usually trading ships—they were entitled to confiscate whatever was on board. At the time, most kingdoms were involved in the practice. The ship's crewmembers received a portion of the gains, and the rest was distributed between the overlords and their kings or queens, according to the hierarchical tradition.

Cabeza de Vaca also participated in two battles in Italy between 1511 and 1513, against French armies. Pope Julius II asked King Ferdinand II of Aragon for help against the French, who were expanding their dominion over the Papal States. King Ferdinand saw an opportunity to expand his own dominion and sent his armies to Italy. In 1511, Cabeza de Vaca sailed from Spain to Naples and in 1512 took part in the Battle of Bologna and in the Battle of Ravenna. The French armies defeated the Spanish armies, and twenty thousand people lost their lives. However, despite this defeat, Cabeza de Vaca was made alférez of Gaeta, a royal standard-bearer, for his outstanding performance in battle.

CHAPTER TWO

LOYALTY PAYS OFF

When Queen Isabella died in 1504, King Ferdinand became head of both major Spanish kingdoms: Aragon and Castile. Cabeza de Vaca returned from the war campaigns in Italy in 1513. Three years later, on January 23, 1516, King Ferdinand died. The direct successor to the Spanish throne was Isabella and Ferdinand's daughter Joan the Mad (Juana la Loca). She inherited the title of Queen of Castile after her mother's death. King Ferdinand's will stated that she should rule the kingdom after his death, but her mental illness made her incapable of doing so. Although she kept the title of queen until her death in 1555, it was her son, together with the king's grandson Charles of Habsburg and the Duke of Burgundy, who

Joan the Mad (Juana la Loca), shown here in a portrait created by Juan de Flandes between 1496 and 1500, became Queen of Castile when her mother, Isabella, died.

exercised the power of Spain. He succeeded to the Spanish throne as Charles I of Aragon and Castile.

FOREIGN KING, A FOREIGN RULE

Charles was proclaimed king in Brussels on March 14, 1516. By this time, he had also inherited the throne of Burgundy and the Netherlands from his father Philip I of Castile. In September 1517, the new king arrived in Spain for the first time. Charles didn't know much about Spain. He had been born in Flanders, today's Belgium, and brought up by his paternal aunt, Margaret of Austria, regent of the Netherlands.

Later in 1519, he inherited the Holy Roman Empire (Germany) from his other grandfather, Maximilian I, at which point he became Charles V (known as Carlos V in Spain). The Holy Roman Emperor ruled not only Spain and his inherited Spanish Crown dominions in Europe and the New World, but also ruled the Netherlands, Austria, and Germany. He became one of the most powerful Christian kings in Europe at the time.

When he arrived in Spain, Charles was not only unfamiliar with Spanish land and culture but also barely spoke the language. Nevertheless, he established new rules in the Spanish kingdom. For example, he allowed Flemish courtiers to dispose of Spanish resources and treasures and use them anywhere else in Europe. He eliminated some privileges enjoyed by Spanish cities and hidalgos, and established new tax codes. Soon, disappointments grew among some Spaniards, who did not like this foreign way of ruling. They wanted to rebel against this king. Soon, they got their chance.

In 1520, while Charles was in Germany, his government in Spain faced a major revolt known as the *comuneros* movement.

This engraving, *Comuneros Revolt,* shows María Pacheco, a noble-woman from the House of Mendoza, leading the rebellion against Charles V's loyal forces in Toledo, Spain.

The comuneros were a group of displeased Castilians that violently revolted against the king and government. Revolts quickly
spread throughout Spain. Cabeza de Vaca and the duke of
Sidonia Medina were among those who steadfastly fought the
comuneros. Fierce battles erupted in Seville when the rebels
took over the city municipal government buildings and the duke's
Alcázar Palace. All the duke's hidalgos, knights, and servants
joined forces to force back the rebels and quickly recaptured the
palace and reinstated government control. Cabeza de Vaca was
in charge of defending the Puerta del Osario, one of the gates in
the encircling wall in the city.

At the same time, Francis I from France saw an opportunity
to invade Spain by way of the territory of Navarra. Many Spanish
hidalgos went to confront the opportunistic French invasion.
The rivalry between these two nations was at an all-time high.
Cabeza de Vaca joined forces in the Battle of Puente de la Reina
(Queen's Bridge) against the French armies. He also battled the
comuneros and recaptured other Spanish cities from the insurgents.

Cabeza de Vaca's unquestionable determination and loyalty
to Charles V were rewarded. He was appointed to the position
of royal treasurer of an ambitious Spanish expedition to the New
World: they would explore, conquer, and settle the portion of the
North American mainland known as La Florida.

King Charles returned to Spain in 1522. By then, the
comuneros revolts were over and the French fought off. The
king reconsidered his previous policies and implemented some
governmental changes. He rewarded his Spanish supporters
with appointments and privileges and replaced all the foreign
appointees in the local governments with Spaniards. In 1524,
he created one of the most important institutions during the
conquering of the Americas: the Royal Council of the Indies. It

SPANISH COLONIAL SETTLEMENTS IN THE NEW WORLD

By 1516, when King Charles took the throne, the Spanish dominions in the New World included the four major Caribbean islands of Hispaniola (today Haiti and Dominican Republic), Cuba, Puerto Rico, and Jamaica. And on Central America's mainland, Spain settled in what is now Panamá. These territories were strategic bases for Spain's exploration of the surrounding lands and islands, as well as a source for basic provisions and Indian laborers. In 1519, the governor of Cuba sent the explorer Hernán Cortés to explore the Yucatán peninsula. In this exploration, Cortés found the great Aztec Empire. Soon after, Cortés broke off with the Cuban governor and claimed the territory for himself. He named this territory New Spain (today México). To avoid retaliations from King Charles, Cortés sent him a letter and gold treasures explaining what he had found and conquered in the name of his majesty.

Hernán Cortés conquered the great Aztec Empire for the Spanish kingdom in just two years. Around 1519, the Aztec Empire's population was about twenty-five million people, according to *Nature* magazine.

administered and governed all Spanish affairs in the Americas. The king's new policies earned the Spaniards' trust, admiration, and respect. However, the king kept governing Spain from other parts of the Holy Empire and disposing Spanish resources elsewhere in Europe.

NAVIGATING WITH NARVÁEZ

From Andalusia in the 1520s, Cabeza de Vaca had probably heard about the events unfolding in the New World. The two *cartas de relación* (letters) that Hernán Cortés sent from New Spain to King Charles were published in Seville in 1522 and 1523. Also in 1522, one of the five ships from the Fernando Magellan and Del Cano global expedition returned to Seville. Many of the stories about the New World could have kindled Cabeza de Vaca's interest in becoming a conqueror, like his father, grandfather, and other family members. He also may have been intrigued by the prospects of fortunes and prestige he could bring himself and his family name.

Cabeza de Vaca's promising adventure began in 1527. The emperor appointed him as the royal treasurer of an expedition authorized to explore, conquer, and settle the territory in North America known as La Florida. He was promised an annual salary of 130,000 *maravedíes*, an ancient Spanish currency, for the term of the expedition. He was asked to deposit 750,000 maravedíes into the royal treasury, however, to guarantee his good behavior while in office. It's unclear how Cabeza de Vaca was able to come up with this large amount of money.

As a royal treasurer, Cabeza de Vaca collected the royal profits, which were resources and treasures acquired during the expedition, such as gold, pearls, precious stones, and slaves.

Pánfilo de Narváez was part of Diego Velásquez's expedition, which conquered Cuba for the Spanish kingdom in 1511. His rivalry with Hernán Cortés was well known.

He was also responsible for paying the salaries of royal officials on the expedition. Additionally, he had to give the emperor an extensive and detailed report on every matter of the expedition, especially about the treatment of the natives, how the royal instructions were accomplished, and about the "teachings of the Indians in the Holy Faith."

Pánfilo de Narváez was the commander of the expedition to La Florida. Narváez was a royal official and wealthy conqueror known for his campaigns in Cuba. He expected to find another Tenochtitlan in North America that would make him as powerful as Cortés in New Spain. Narváez was authorized to conquer and to serve as governor of all the territory he could bring under Spanish control. Although he didn't receive any royal funding to finance his expedition, he was promised a salary of 250,000 maravedíes for the rest of his life.

On June 17, 1527, Narváez's five ships, carrying six hundred men, embarked from the port of San Lúcar de Barrameda, Andalusia. Cabeza de Vaca was on his first journey to the New World.

CHAPTER THREE

EXPLORING, CONQUERING, AND POPULATING LA FLORIDA

The notion Spaniards had of La Florida territory was more extensive than the Florida Peninsula we know today. The territory of La Florida included the region surrounding the Gulf and from the Pacific to the Atlantic Oceans. New Spain was already under Spanish control by Hernán Cortés, and its north side was unconquered. Narváez's expedition wanted to take over as much of the unexplored land as possible. That portion of territory included what are now the states of Texas, Louisiana, Mississippi, Alabama, and Florida. Moreover, because the plan was to explore and conquer from coast to coast, it also included today's states of California, Arizona, and New México.

FIRST STOPS: HISPANIOLA AND CUBA

The Narváez expedition's first stop was Santo Domingo, in Hispaniola, around September 17, 1527. The company stayed for about forty-five days, gathering provisions and another ship, bringing the fleet's total to six ships. Horses were one of the most valuable provisions for transportation. Because horses did not exist in the New World before Spaniards arrived with them, Indians feared these strange, unknown creatures.

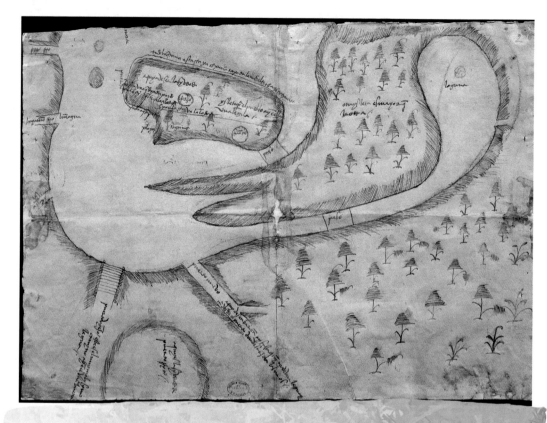

The sailors on the Narváez expedition may have used a map of Puerto Rico and Santo Domingo like this one from around 1519 to find Santo Domingo's port.

While in Santo Domingo, 140 men deserted the expedition. Apparently, they were frightened off by scary stories about the Indians in La Florida.

From Santo Domingo, the remaining expedition headed to the town of Trinidad, in Cuba, for more provisions. On the way, Narváez decided to stop in Cabo de Santa Cruz with four of the ships. He sent two ships to Trinidad with Cabeza de Vaca and Captain Juan Pantoja to restock necessary provisions for the expedition.

THE MAPS OF THE NEW WORLD

When Cabeza de Vaca went to the New World, the conquerors had only two maps to go by. The first map, known as the Pineda map, was sent to the Spanish royal court in 1519, and the second was sent by Hernán Cortés in 1522. Both maps showed the Gulf area, from Yucatan to Florida. These maps were mostly inaccurate, however; the real distances were longer in reality and many land details had been missed.

Curiously, the maps showed the Florida peninsula as an island. Juan Ponce de León, the first European to report about Florida in 1513, thought he had discovered an island, and that was how it was recorded on the first maps. He named it Florida to honor the Spanish Easter season, known in Spain as Pascua Florida, or Feast of Flowers.

Cabeza de Vaca and Pantoja arrived in Trinidad on a Friday in the late afternoon. Pantoja and some men hiked about 3 miles (5 kilometers) inland to the town. Cabeza de Vaca and the others remained with the ships. According to Cabeza de Vaca's story, he had been warned that many vessels had been lost in this dangerous port. They needed to guard the ships and then depart as soon as possible.

The next morning, rain started to fall and signs of bad weather were all around. Later, the winds howled and the weather worsened. Twice that day Trinidad residents begged Cabeza de Vaca to come to town. He refused. Finally, he agreed to go help get supplies so they all could leave the port sooner. Only an hour after he headed to town, he wrote in *Relación*, "the sea began to rise ominously and the north wind blow so violently that the two boats would not have dared come near land." The storm raged for two days, destroying trees and houses. When it was safe for Cabeza de Vaca to return back to shore the ships were gone! Only a small boat was found—in a treetop. About sixty people lost their lives. The only survivors were those who went to town.

Narváez later arrived in Trinidad with four sturdy boats. Everyone was so traumatized from the storm that they didn't want to sail in wintertime. The Trinidadians supported their decision and advised them to wait. Cabeza de Vaca took the crew and the ships to a safe port in Jagua, in the Bay of Cienfuegos, Cuba. They remained there until February 20, 1528.

LANDING IN FLORIDA

In April 1528, ten months after leaving Spain, the expedition

The Narváez expedition faced several sea storms during their journey to conquer La Florida. The harrowing experiences made the sailors wary of setting sail in winter, so they waited.

first sighted Florida. Florida was an unknown territory, or *terra incognita*. The three known previous expeditions didn't give a detailed description. Thus, Cabeza de Vaca's Relación became the very first European written account of this land and its peoples.

After spending two days in search of a suitable harbor, the expedition anchored somewhere in Tampa Bay. From the ships, Cabeza de Vaca wrote, "We could see some houses and habitations of Indians" made of wood and thatch. Alonso Enríquez, an official from the expedition, went to meet the Indians. Cabeza de Vaca wrote that the natives and Enríquez spent some time "trading fish and venison for European trinkets."

The next day, the Spanish arrived at a deserted village. The Native Americans had left in the night by canoe. Cabeza de Vaca described one of the houses as big enough to hold three hundred people, but the rest were smaller. Narváez took possession of the land in the name of the Spanish crown, raised the flags, and set up a base camp. A day later, however, the Native Americans returned. They used gestures to communicate, but the Spaniards didn't understand what they meant. Cabeza de Vaca felt that the Indians' many gestures were threats indicating that they wanted the Spaniards to leave. But eventually, the Indians gave up and left the Spaniards alone.

Narváez worried that their food supply was running low. Then, he, Cabeza de Vaca, and others went in search of food along the shore of the bay. There, they found several shipwrecks. And they also found gold! Narváez quickly changed his interest from finding food to gold. With the gold in his hands, he went back to the Native Americans. Using gestures, Narváez asked them where to find more of it. The Native Americans led him to a village they called Apalachee—after the name of the tribe—where there "was much gold and plenty of everything we wanted," wrote Cabeza de Vaca.

This must have made sense to these men because they thought they had landed near New Spain (Mexico) where Hernán Cortés had found the great city of Tenochtitlan, full of gold and treasures. Little did they know that they were many miles away from the Aztec Empire.

Against Cabeza de Vaca's strong objections, Narváez divided the company in two groups. One group would sail along the coast and the other would follow him over land toward the Apalachee's village. Cabeza de Vaca worried that the two groups would lose track of one another. The ship captains were also unsure of their exact location, but they were afraid to contradict Narváez. Cabeza de Vaca proposed that they stick together, find a secure port to camp, and from there explore overland. He didn't get support, though, so they all followed Narváez's command.

The Spaniard explorers traveled through a landscape they had never seen or experienced before. The Indian captives may have tried to lead them through the most difficult passages.

THE APALACHEE ADVENTURE

The overland group, which included Narváez, packed up their gear and set off toward the Apalachee with a few Indian captives as guides. In his report, Cabeza de Vaca said they came across many lagoons, deer, enormous trees, and low palm trees called palmettos, much like those of Castile. He also noticed the soil was sandy and stiff. Throughout the journey, the natives repeatedly attacked them with arrows. Finally, they saw an Apalachee village, which Narváez ordered Cabeza de Vaca and his soldiers to attack.

When they arrived, there wasn't much to attack: they found only women and children, and a cornfield. They searched the village of forty houses but found no men or gold anywhere. It was theirs to occupy. Soon the Indian men returned, however, and fought the Spanish intruders. When they couldn't beat them and had retreated, the cacique (chief) and a small delegation approached the Spaniards in hopes of negotiating, but instead Narváez took the chief as a hostage. While the Spaniards remained in the village feeding themselves, Cabeza de Vaca took notes about the Native American habits and farming, as well as the flora and fauna of the area. In the meantime, the Native American men watched the village from the outside, repeatedly attacking the Spaniards in hopes of freeing their cacique and forcing out the intruders.

OUT OF THE APALACHEE TERRITORY

One day, the chief persuaded the Spaniards to go south. There they would find the sea and the village of Aute. In Aute, he said, there was enough maize, beans, squash, and fish to feed all. The Spaniards all agreed and walked for nine days through swamps, lagoons, and rivers. All along the way, the natives attacked, leaving Cabeza de Vaca with a minor wound. When

It is hard to imagine all the struggles Cabeza de Vaca and other Spanish explorers experienced in their journey through La Florida. This commemorative sign is a reminder.

they finally arrived, Aute was abandoned. The Indians must have known they were coming and left.

Cabeza de Vaca set off to find the sea and look for their ships, on Narváez's orders. All he found were coves and bays, however, with neither open sea nor ships to be found.

Meanwhile in Aute, many Spaniards fell ill, including Narváez. Finally, desperate to escape constant attacks from the Native Americans, they all left the village and camped in the Río de la Magdalena. (The actual location of the river is unknown, but the Aucilla, St. Marks, and Ochlockonee Rivers all drain into the Apalachee Bay, or La Bahía de Caballos [Bay of Horses] as the Spaniards called it.)

At this point, many men and horses had been lost in battles. Several men were seriously ill. Moreover, they still had no idea where their ships were, and everyone wanted to leave. They finally decided to build barges and try to reach a Spanish outpost, either at Santisteban del Puerto on the Río Pánuco or Río de las Palmas, both in the northern side of New Spain (Mexico). Finally, they had a plan.

CHAPTER FOUR

LOST AND OUTCASTS

In September 1528, five barges carrying 242 men launched into the Apalachee Bay. For seven days, they rowed toward the open sea. Hungry, thirsty, and losing hope of survival, they sailed westward close to the coast. In *Relación*, Cabeza de Vaca wrote: "Considering where we were and how little hope we had of relief, you may sufficiently imagine our sufferings."

Eventually, some compassionate natives reached out and gave them temporary shelter, food, and water. But soon, Native Americans attacked them again. The desperate Spaniards had no choice but to return to their barges and continue by water.

ENCOUNTERING THE MISSISSIPPI RIVER

For several days, Cabeza de Vaca led the five barges along the coast. They eventually caught sight of a large river, which must have been the Mississippi River. Narváez's group of barges anchored nearby on the mainland. When Cabeza de Vaca tried to approach them, a strong current and a northern wind pushed his barge out to sea.

Unable to reach the coast, Cabeza de Vaca and his men continued sailing westward. After a few days, they saw two barges and approached the nearest one. In it was Narváez, who asked Cabeza de Vaca what they should do. Cabeza de Vaca suggested attaching the three barges so they could continue together. But once again Narváez disagreed. Cabeza de Vaca recorded in *Relación* that the commander told him "that it was no longer a time when one should command another; that each must do as he thought best to save himself; that that was what he was doing now." So Narváez's barges left on their own.

Later in his journey through what is now the state of Texas, Cabeza de Vaca learned Narváez's fate. The leader's barge disappeared somewhere close to the Matagorda Peninsula. He had been sleeping on his barge ill, thin, and with a leprous disease on his skin. According to the story, during the night, a north wind hit and pushed the barge into the dark sea, never to be seen again.

MALHADO ISLAND

Cabeza de Vaca's barge continued sailing alone for several more days. Everyone was exhausted and disoriented. One day, before dawn, a huge wave took his barge and pushed it to shore. There, they made a fire, ate, and drank fresh water. They began to revive. Cabeza de Vaca recorded these events as happening on November 6, 1528. He had no idea where they were, but based on his descriptions, they were probably in what is now Texas, near Galveston Island. They called this island Isla de Malhado, or Isle of Evil Fate.

Exploring a trail, they found an empty Native American village. They took the food they found and returned to shore. Later that day, hundreds of natives surrounded the Spaniards on the beach. All were male, tall, and well formed according to Cabeza de Vaca. Courageously, the royal treasurer approached the

Native Americans and offered bells and beads. In return, wrote Cabeza de Vaca, the natives gave them an arrow as a "sign of friendship" and invited them to their village. Cabeza de Vaca and some others moved to the camp. Others declined, in fear of being killed.

In the village, Cabeza de Vaca found two different tribes: the Capoques and the Hans. The Indians subsisted by hunting and gathering. But the winter of 1528–1529 was harsh and food was scarce for all. Many Indians and Spaniards fell ill, and several of them died.

Cabeza de Vaca observed how the "Indian medicine-men," as he called them, healed the sick with herbs and hot stones. It took several years for Cabeza de Vaca to figure out the Indians' healing practice, but he eventually started practicing medicine in 1535.

The surviving Spaniards remained with the Native Americans on Malhado Island for about four years. Some Spaniards from the expedition left the group, but most were eventually captured by other Native Americans. The Spaniards were always looking to reach a route southbound to the Spanish outpost on the Río Pánuco, so they occasionally crossed paths. Many were separated when they took different routes, died of starvation and cold, joined Native American groups, or simply disappeared.

IN NEW SPAIN

Cabeza de Vaca, Dorantes, Castillo, and the slave Estevanico were the four last survivors from the Narváez expedition in La Florida. They finally met again when different Native American groups came together to harvest a region during the prickly pear season, in today's southwest Texas. The four joined the

Cabeza de Vaca would not have survived wandering through unknown lands without the Indians. He learned their languages, customs, and survival practices.

Avavares tribe and continued traveling southbound when they could. But they switched locations and groups several times, through which they learned different Native American languages, customs, and healing practices. Their experience as healers gained protection and respect from the Indians.

During the journey, Cabeza de Vaca encountered a group he called the "cow people." They introduced him to the American bison, or buffalo. Cabeza de Vaca had never seen such an animal before. He offered the first European description of it. He called it vaca, or cow, for its similarity. This event probably happened during the buffalo-hunting season in late summer or early autumn of 1535.

REUNITED AND HOME AGAIN

One morning, Cabeza de Vaca and his companions saw traces of horses not far from their camp, close by Río Petatlán (known as Río Sinaloa today). Cabeza de Vaca was sure Spaniards were nearby. They immediately sought them out. It took a few days, but they found their fellow Spaniards. Cabeza de Vaca

THE TEXAS INDIAN GROUPS

Later in *Relación*, Cabeza de Vaca writes that he had encountered twenty-three Indian groups throughout his journey across Texas. He classified these groups into three categories: those who spent part of each year on the offshore islands, those who lived on the mainland shore, and those who lived farther inland. Among those living in the islands were the Capoques and Hans of Malhado, the Deaguanes, Quevenes, Guaycones, Camones, and the People of the Figs. The People of the Figs probably lived on Padre Island. Among the shoreline groups he included the Charrucos, who lived in the Galveston Bay region, Mendicas Mariames, Yguases, and Quitoles. In the third category living inland were the Avavares, Atayos, Acubadaos, Eanagados, Cuthalchuches, Maliacones, Coayos, Susolas, Arbadaos, Cuchendados, and Comos. All were nomadic peoples.

may have been shocked to learn it was 1536. Throughout his travels, he had lost track of time: eight years had passed since he left Spain.

After meeting up with the other Spaniards, Alvar Núñez Cabeza de Vaca, Alonso del Castillo Maldonado, Andrés Dorantes, and Estevanico soon traveled to Mexico, then the capital of New Spain. They arrived on Sunday, July 23, 1536. The four survivors were welcomed with great hospitality and honors by Viceroy de Mendoza and Hernán Cortés. Cabeza de Vaca departed for Spain in 1537.

DEPARTING FOR RIO DE LA PLATA

Back in Spain, Cabeza de Vaca had planned to ask for a royal appointment in Florida as governor. However, Hernando de Soto was already appointed as governor and commander of an expedition to Florida. De Soto tried his best to hire Cabeza de Vaca, but Cabeza de Vaca declined. He didn't want to risk suffering the consequences of another's incompetence and foolish decisions again. He wanted to be a first commander and governor himself.

Charles V offered Cabeza de Vaca an alternate appointment: the government of the Rio de la Plata province, a rich region in South America in today's Paraguay. The Rio de la Plata colony was in a state of unrest. The indigenous population was suffering from the abuses of the acting governor, Juan de Ayolas. Many diseases were spreading, and

Cabeza de Vaca traveled barefoot through the magnificent Iguazú Falls and the surrounding rain forest to reach the city of Asunción, in Paraguay.

Asunción, the colony capital, was wasting away. Cabeza de Vaca departed for Rio de la Plata in 1540.

On his arrival, Cabeza de Vaca chose to lead the expedition overland toward Asunción. They crossed 1,000 miles (1,609 kilometers) of unknown jungles, mountains, and cannibal villages—all while barefoot! Their trek lasted from November 1541 to March 1542. They traveled from Santa Catalina Island via Iguazú Falls to Asunción. The following summer, Cabeza de Vaca tried to find the legendary Golden City of Manoa in Paraguay, but extreme weather conditions prevented him.

Back in Asunción, the Spaniards were disappointed with the way Cabeza de Vaca was ruling. He prohibited enslaving, abusing, and looting the Native Americans, unlike most Spaniards. So they conspired against Cabeza de Vaca and sent him back to Spain in chains in 1543. In Spain, the Council of the Indies sentenced Cabeza de Vaca to deportation to Africa for eight years. His loyal wife spent her fortune on his behalf during the long-lasting trials.

Finally, the plots against Cabeza de Vaca were revealed, and the king annulled his sentence. He was awarded a pension and a position in the royal court. Álvar Núñez Cabeza de Vaca died with honor in 1557.

A LEGACY OF WRITING AND RESPECT

Cabeza de Vaca's major legacy is the written accounts of his explorations and encounters in the New World. His records have become a basis for North American and South American history. Most important, he also wrote about his own, very

IV CENTENARIO DE
FLORIDA
1 PTA
CABEZA DE VACA
CORREOS
ESPAÑA

In 1960, the Spanish post office printed this stamp honoring Álvar Núñez Cabeza de Vaca, commemorating the four hundredth anniversary of the discovery and colonization of La Florida.

human impressions, including his struggles to understand and learn from a very different world.

His narrative also shows his determination to change the barbaric European approach to colonizing the Americas. He was among those who tried to set strict rules for respecting the indigenous peoples and their cultures in the colonies. During his time in the New World, Álvar Núñez Cabeza de Vaca succeeded in establishing peaceful relationships with the Indians and gaining their appreciation and friendship, a rare approach in the many stories of exploration, and a voice that should not be forgotten.

TIMELINE

1469 King Ferdinand II of Aragón and Queen Isabella I of Castile marry.

1485–1495 Approximate range for Álvar Núñez Cabeza de Vaca's birth date.

1492 Christopher Columbus discovers the New World. The Spaniards recapture the last Muslim settlement in Spain, ending seven hundred years of the Reconquista wars.

1503 Cabeza de Vaca begins his service to the House of Medina Sidonia.

1511–1513 Cabeza de Vaca goes to Italy to fight the French armies. He's made alferez of Gaeta.

June 17, 1527 Cabeza de Vaca embarks on Narváez expedition to conquer La Florida.

September 17, 1527 Narváez expedition arrives in Santo Domingo and sails to Cuba.

April 1528 Narváez expedition departs from Cuba and lands on the Florida peninsula.

1528 The Spanish expedition meets the Apalachee and other Florida Indians. The expedition loses its ships and launches barges into Apalachee Bay. They arrive at Malhado Island, but Narváez deserts.

1529–1536 Cabeza de Vaca wanders the rim of the Gulf of Mexico to Texas. He joins different Native American groups and becomes a medicine man. He finds other Spaniards and finally goes to Mexico.

1537 Cabeza de Vaca arrives back in Spain. King Charles V appoints him to govern the province of Rio de la Plata in South America.

1540 Cabeza de Vaca departs for Rio de la Plata in his second appointment to the New World.

1543–1551 A plot against Cabeza de Vaca sends him in chains back to Spain. He's sentenced to deportation to Africa for eight years. The Council of the Indies reveals the plot and annuls the sentence.

1557–1559 Cabeza de Vaca dies, probably in Jerez de la Frontera or Seville, Spain.

GLOSSARY

barge A rustic large boat, usually flat at the bottom, used on inland waters like rivers or channels and moved by towing.

chamberlain A chief official in charge of the house of a king, queen, or noble person.

colony A territory or country controlled and governed by another country.

confiscate To remove others' belongings or rights legally.

conquistador A historical Spanish figure and leader in the American conquest during the sixteenth century.

converso A Jewish person who abandoned his Jewish faith and adopted Christianity by force in Europe during the fifteenth century.

courtier A person in charge of an official position in a king's or queen's court.

epic A long story that tells the adventures and misadventures of a hero or historical figure.

Flemish A person and language originally from Flanders, in northern Belgium, known today as Dutch.

hidalgo A minor noble in Spain.

Holy Faith The Christian faith promoted by the Holy Roman Empire in Europe and the Americas.

Holy Roman Empire The historical empire made of several territories in Europe that lasted from the ninth or tenth century until 1806.

Indian An original native of the Americas. As Christopher Columbus thought he had arrived in India, the people he found were called Indians.

insurgent A person who fights against an established social order or government.

journey A long-distance trek or trip.

lineage A noble family line of ancestors and descendants.

maravedíes A medieval currency used in Spain.

Moor An African Muslim person who conquered Spain.

New Spain A Spanish viceroyalty, or authority, from 1535 to 1823 over North America, Central America, the West Indies, and the Philippines.

New World A term Europeans used to name the unknown territories of North, Central, and South America in the fifteenth century.

noble A titled member of a kingdom, such as duke, hidalgo, king, or queen.

social hierarchy An organizational form of categorizing a group of people in a society that determines access to some privileges or not.

successor A person who comes after another and is now in charge of a throne, a title, an estate, or an office.

thatch A covering made of straw, leaves, or other natural material.

FOR MORE INFORMATION

Canadian Historical Association
1912-130 Albert Street
Ottawa, ON K1P 5G4
Canada
(613) 233-7885
Email: cha-shc@cha-shc.ca
Website: http://www.cha-shc.ca
Twitter: @CndHistAssoc
The Canadian Historical
Association is a bilingual
(English and French) orga-
nization, supporting and
encouraging the study of,
communication about, and
inquiry about historical
topics among all people
around the world.

Hispanic Society of America
613 West 155th Street
New York, NY 10032
(212) 926 2234
Email: info@hispanicsociety.org
Website: www.hispanicsociety
.org
Facebook and Instagram:
@hispanicsociety
Twitter: @HSAmuseum
YouTube: Hispanic Society
Museum & Library
The Hispanic Society of

America is a free public
museum and library. Its
collection includes works
from countries where
Spanish and Portuguese
are or were predominant
languages: Spain, Portugal,
Latin America, and the
Philippines.

Instituto Cervantes
31 W. Ohio
Chicago, IL 60654
(312) 335-1996
Websites: http://www
.cervantesvirtual.com
http://www.chicago.cervantes
.es/en/default.shtm
Facebook and Instagram:
@Instituto.Cervantes
.Chicago
Twitter: @Chicago_IC
The Instituto Cervantes was
created to promote Spanish
language and Hispanic
American culture around
the world.

National Hispanic Cultural Center
1701 4th Street SW
Albuquerque, NM 87102

(505) 246 2261
Email: NHCC.Info@state.nm.us
Website: http://www.nhccnm
.org
Facebook, Twitter, and
Instagram: @NHCCNM
The National Hispanic Cultural
Center is dedicated to
supporting and promoting
Hispanic culture, arts, and
humanities. It includes an
art museum, a library, a
genealogy center, and educational resources open to
the public.

**Texas State Historical
Association (TSHA)**
3001 Lake Austin Boulevard,
Suite 3.116
Austin, TX 78703
(512) 471 2600
Website: http://www.tshaonline
.org/home
Facebook: @TexasStateHis-
toricalAssociation
Twitter: @TxStHistAssoc
The Texas State Historical
Association is dedicated to
promoting and preserving
the history and culture of
Texas and all things related

to the state. It also supports
educational programs for
elementary through college
students through its website
as well as in schools.

**Wisconsin Historical Society/
American Journeys**
816 State Street
Madison, WI 53706
(608) 264 6535
Email: asklibrary
@wisconsinhistory.org
Websites: http://www
.americanjourneys.org
http://www.wisconsinhistory.org
Facebook: @
wisconsinhistoricalsociety
Twitter: @WisHistory
The American Journeys website includes accounts of
North American explo-
ration. It's free and very
useful for school research
on these topics.

FOR FURTHER READING

Conklin, Wendy. *Finding Florida: Explorations and Its Legacy.* Huntington Beach, CA: Teacher Created Materials, 2017.

Farndon, John, and Christian Cornia. *The Middle Ages: New Conquests and Dynasties* (Human History Timeline). Minneapolis, MN: Lerner Publishing Group, 2018.

Hayes, Amy. *Native Peoples of the Southwest.* New York, NY: Gareth Stevens Publishing, 2016.

Johnston, Lissa. *Crossing a Continent: The Incredible Journey of Cabeza De Vaca.* Leesville, SC: Lissa Johnston, 2016.

Kallen, Stuart A. *A Journey with Francisco Vázquez de Coronado.* Minneapolis, MN: Lerner Publishing Group, 2018.

Murray, Margaret C. Spiral: *A Novel of the Ancient Southwest.* Pinole, CA: WriteWords Press, 2015.

Nussbaum, Ben. *Junípero Serra: A Spanish Missionary.* Huntington Beach, CA: Teacher Created Materials, 2017.

Owens, Lisa L. *A Journey with Hernán Cortés* (Primary Source Explorers). Minneapolis, MN: Lerner Publishing Group, 2018.

Peppas, Lynn. *Why Cabeza de Vaca Matters to Texas* (Texas Perspectives). New York, NY: Rosen Classroom, 2013.

Russell, Sharman A. *Teresa of the New World.* New York, NY: Yucca Publishing, 2015.

BIBLIOGRAPHY

Adorno, Rolena, and Patrick Charles Pautz. "Introduction." In *The Narrative of Cabeza de Vaca*, 1–25. University of Nebraska Press, 2003. https://books.google.com /books?id=jxsR83VZc84C&printsec=frontcover&source=gbs _ViewAPI&hl=en#v=onepage&q&f=false.

Andrews, Evan. "Stranded in the New World: The Amazing Odyssey of Cabeza de Vaca." History Stories, April 28, 2017. http://www.history.com/news/stranded-in-the-new-world-the -amazing-odyssey-of-cabeza-de-vaca.

Bandelier, Adolph Francis. "Alvar Nuñez Cabeza de Vaca." New Advent. Robert Appleton Company. Retrieved February 27, 2018. http://www.newadvent.org/cathen/03126c.htm.

Bandalier, Adolph Francis, ed. "The Journey of Alvar Nuñez Cabeza de Vaca." American Journeys. 2018. http://www .americanjourneys.org/aj-070/summary.

Boyd, Andy. "Cabeza de Vaca: An Alternative Vision for the Settling of America." U.S. History Scene. Retrieved February 27, 2018. http://ushistoryscene.com/article/de-vaca.

Cabeza De Vaca, Álvar Núñez. *The Journey and Ordeal of Cabeza de Vaca: His Account of the Disastrous First European Exploration of the American Southwest*. Translated and edited by Cyclone Covey. New York, NY: Dover Publications, 2003.

Chipman, Donald E. "Cabeza de Vaca, Álvar Núñez." *Handbook of Texas Online*. August 3, 2017. http://www.tshaonline.org /handbook/online/articles/fca06.

Grant, Richard. "Cabeza de Vaca." Cowboys Indians, August/ September 2015. http://www.cowboysindians.com/2015/08 /cabeza-de-vaca.

Moguer, M. "Álvar Núñez Cabeza de Vaca, el descubridor que pasó seis años desnudo en América." ABC de Seville. August

21, 2013. http://seville.abc.es/seville/20130821/sevi-alvar
-nunez-cabeza-201308141512.html.

New Perspectives on the West. "Alvar Nuñez Cabeza de Vaca."
PBS, September 1996. Retrieved February 27, 2018. http://
www.pbs.org/weta/thewest/people/a_c/cabezadevaca.htm.

Rivas, José Andrés. "El último viaje de Alvar Núñez Cabeza
de Vaca." Biblioteca Virtual Miguel de Cervantes. Retrieved
February 27, 2018. http://www.cervantesvirtual.com
/obra-visor/el-ultimo-viaje-de-alvar-nunez-cabeza-de-vaca
/html/5f8c321c-6a9d-4d0f-895d-e4047235e4c9_2.html#I_0.

Torres Ramírez, Bibiano. Álvar Núñez Cabeza de Vaca. Seville,
Spain: Editoriales Andaluzas Unidas, 1990.

Varnum, Robin. *Álvar Nuñez Cabeza de Vaca: American
Trailblazer.* Norman, OK: University of Oklahoma Press, 2014.

Varnum, Robin. "Cabeza de Vaca: An Unlikely Hero for Native
Americans." Signature. Penguin Random House, October 24,
2014. http://www.signature-reads.com/2014/10/cabeza-de
-vaca-the-unlikely-explorer-who-defended-native-americans.

INDEX

ABOUT THE AUTHOR

Sandra Colmenares has been writing and editing books for thirty years. Her passion for books, research, and knowledge on a myriad of subjects started at an early age, while spending time with her mother, a respected Venezuelan librarian and educator, at the National Library of Venezuela in Caracas. Colmenares's curiosity for knowledge and books led her to complete a BA in Letras at Universidad Central de Venezuela. After moving to the United States in 1997, she continued her career as an editor, writer, researcher, and translator in education and media on exceptional art, literary, and historical figures.

PHOTO CREDITS